Anxiety

Techniques For Transforming Stress And Escaping Anxiety So You Can Stay Motivated And Take Control Of Your Career

(A Powerful Method Based On The Body That Can Help You Conquer Anxiety And Find Relief From Fear And Worry)

Armando Carbajal

TABLE OF CONTENT

Even Our Hormones Have A Hand To Play In The Process. 1

Conquering A Particular Aversion 6

Understanding The Signs Of Anxiety In Teens ..9

Different Categories Of Overthinking 13

Strategies For Avoiding Or Putting An End To Excessive Or Unnecessary Pondering 18

The Significance Of Having A High Level Of Emotional Intelligence 26

Embracing The Strength That Comes From Motion 29

Self-Evaluation Activities To Help You Gain A Better Understanding Of Your Attachment Style 34

Embracing Your Own Needs And Caring For Yourself 53

Practicing Regular Activities Can Provide Long-Term Relief From Anxiety 56

Strategies For Avoiding Anxiety As A Preventive Measure 60

The Relationship That Exists Between One's Thinking, Feelings, And Actions 72

Recognize Any And All Cognitive Fractionations 76

Cbt Methods For The Treatment Of Anxiety 83

Activities Performed On A Daily Basis That Contribute To The Preservation Of Mental And Emotional Health 86

Improving One's Social Skills: A Roadmap To One's Own Personal And Professional Development 89

Investigating How Attention Deficit Hyperactivity Disorder Can Affect Intimacy And Relationship Bonding 106

Letting Go Of Mental Attachments And Detachements In Order To Release Them 114

Understanding Anxiety Through Both Art And Science 143

Share What You Have To Offer With The World. 148

Debunked Theories About Anxiety 152

Putting Together Your Personal Protection Strategy 157

: Practice Gratitude 162

Both The Cortex And The Amygdala Are Involved. 164

Even Our Hormones Have A Hand To Play In The Process.

When it comes to hormones, there are primarily two perspectives that one can take. To start, women are more likely than men to go through significant hormonal shifts on a regular basis. For instance, pregnancy is one of these events that might cause changes in hormone levels. In a similar manner, our menstrual cycles can cause variations in our hormone levels every month. Because hormones can alter both mood and behavior, it stands to reason that they can also affect the symptoms of social anxiety disorder. In this context, we are concerned with three different kinds of hormones: stress hormones, thyroid hormones, and sexual hormones.

Cortisol and adrenaline are two hormones that are produced in increased quantities by our bodies in response to high levels of stress. When we are under a tremendous deal of stress, our lives can become extremely stressful. Cortisol is the principal hormone that is secreted in response to stress, whereas adrenaline is the hormone that is secreted when the body is in a state of "fight or flight." When we are confronted with a genuine danger in our life, these hormones prove to be of great assistance. On the other hand, if we consistently believe that we are in danger, our systems may produce an excessive amount of these hormones, which may result in an increase in the severity of our anxiety feelings. Because social anxiety can be experienced on a daily basis, it can lead to a vicious cycle in which excessive anxiety caused by perceived threats can promote the overproduction of certain hormones, which can then produce additional anxiety. Since social anxiety can be experienced on a regular basis, it can also lead to increased anxiety. Studies have shown that women are more prone to rumination, which indicates that they focus on negative ideas more than males do. While there are numerous reasons why someone could experience stress, studies have also shown that there are various reasons why someone might experience stress. According to Johnson and Whisman (2013), placing an excessive amount of emphasis on such ideas almost always results in an increase in levels of stress and anxiety.

Testosterone and estrogen are the two primary hormones that are involved in sexual activity. According to the findings of certain studies, having low amounts of either testosterone or estrogen can raise our feelings of anxiety. Additionally, the production of the hormone cortisol, generally known as the stress hormone, and testosterone are connected to one another in some way. For instance, having high levels of cortisol in our systems can bring about decreased amounts of testosterone, and having low levels of testosterone can also bring about an increase in cortisol levels automatically. As you can see, this results in another cycle in which stress hormones and sex hormones together can cause you to feel nervous all the time (Cuncic, 2020b).

Because of the role that sex hormones play in the regulation of our menstrual cycles, puberty, pregnancy, and the menopause, we are more likely to experience feelings of anxiety during these life transitions.

The hormones produced by the thyroid are the third type of hormone that may be contributing to our social anxiety. When our thyroid hormones are created in greater quantities, they have the potential to contribute to a variety of physiological symptoms, including trembling, an accelerated heart rate and palpitations, as well as profuse sweating. These symptoms could, in turn, make the behaviors associated with your social anxiety worse.

The good news is that your hormones might also be responsible for reducing the symptoms of anxiety you're experiencing. For instance, research has shown that having higher amounts of both testosterone and estrogen can help people feel less anxious and more in control of their emotions. Vasopressin and oxytocin are two more hormones that have been shown to be effective in the treatment of anxiety. The hormone vasopressin has been linked to sexual drive, pair bonding, maternal stress responses, and social behavior. Oxytocin is commonly referred to as the "love hormone" due to the fact that it is secreted during physical contact between mother and child, during hugs, and in other situations in which we experience a sense of being loved and secure. Oxytocin is a hormone that naturally occurs in our systems. Having higher levels of oxytocin in our bodies can help us feel more calm in social settings, which can help minimize feelings of social anxiety.

Conquering A Particular Aversion

Consider what your primary objective is. The question is, why haven't you finished it yet? If you're like most others, the solution is probably something as simple as fear.

Fear is the limiting factor that is preventing you from advancing toward what it is that you want. Fear causes us to lose focus and makes us more likely to make excuses, but it doesn't have to.

One of the most liberating things you can do with your time is to educate yourself on how to prevail over your fears.

It is simple to fool yourself into believing that fear is not holding you back and to come up with reasons why you haven't completed what you are capable of doing.

Rather than running away and hiding from the threat, you should utilize your fear as a motivator to take action and not as an excuse.

Take a look at your end goal. You have conceded if you give in to your fears and let them prevent you from achieving your goals.

The limiting beliefs that are holding you back are the source of many of your fears, including the fear of the unknown, the fear of failing, and other common worries.

THE MENTAL PROCESSES Involved in Conquering Fear

If you don't understand the fundamental ideas behind overcoming fear and anxiety, learning how to do so could seem like a terrifying prospect.

Before you start berating yourself for feeling worried, it's important to realize that fear is a natural and usual response that evolved over time.

Even if it might not appear that way at the time, your brain and body are always trying to communicate with you.

Conquering a fear becomes much simpler after one has gained an understanding of the indicators of that fear.

Fear is more than the physical manifestations that we frequently experience in response to stressful situations. There are many different kinds of fear, and some of them are far more harmful.

Understanding The Signs Of Anxiety In Teens

Teenagers are complicated individuals, and the events that they go through might sometimes be buried in enigma. To understand worry in teenagers, one needs to have a perceptive eye and a compassionate heart. In this chapter, we are going to go deeper into the signs and symptoms of teen anxiety, investigate the impact of social media and technology, and reveal the delicate connection between physical and mental health.

The Signs and Symptoms Section Comes First

It's important to detect the subtle and not-so-subtle indicators of anxiety in teenagers because they don't always verbalize their feelings and challenges, and it's also important to note when they do. The following is a list of frequent indications and symptoms that you should keep an eye out for:

Teens who suffer from anxiety are more likely to have physical symptoms such as headaches, stomachaches, muscle tightness, and exhaustion. These outward manifestations are frequently the body's method of reacting to the stress that it is experiencing.

Mood Swings Anxiety can cause a person's emotions to swing wildly from moment to moment. It is not uncommon for adolescents to develop a short fuse, become quickly agitated, or worry excessively about mundane matters. Mood swings and an increased tendency to cry may both be signs that there is underlying anxiety.

Changes in Behavior: Keep an eye out for any shifts in behavior. It may be an indication of anxiety if a person avoids social events, their homework, or their duties. Some adolescents may become disinterested in activities that they previously enjoyed.

Sleep Disturbances Anxiety frequently causes sleep patterns to be thrown off. It's not uncommon for adolescents to have problems getting asleep, trouble remaining asleep, or recurrent nightmares. Anxiety symptoms might be made worse by not getting enough sleep.

Academic Obstacles: A deterioration in academic achievement, especially in individuals who are otherwise talented, can be a warning sign. Anxiety can make it difficult to concentrate, which in turn can impair memory and one's ability to finish activities.

Isolation from Society: Adolescents who struggle with anxiety may pull away from their friends and other social activities, opting for solitude rather than face potential social stressors. They can be worried that their peers will judge or criticize them.

Perfectionism is a form of anxiousness that disguises itself as a desire for perfection. Teenagers sometimes have overly high expectations for themselves because they are afraid of the repercussions that come with falling short.

Fidgeting or Restlessness in the Body
Fidgeting or restlessness in the body is a common coping mechanism for worried energy that some adolescents exhibit. This can show itself as chewing the nails, spinning the hair, or shaking the legs.

The first step in assisting adolescents in dealing with their anxiety is to assist them in recognizing these signs and symptoms. It is absolutely necessary to approach them with empathy and open dialogue, so establishing a secure environment in which they may freely share their thoughts, feelings, and concerns.

Different Categories Of Overthinking

Two of the most common manifestations of too much thinking, also known as overthinking, are dwelling on the past and being anxious about the future.

When they do so, certain people are engaging in the cognitive distortion known as overthinking. Cognitive distortions, also known as faulty thought patterns, can be the root of mental health issues such as anxiety, stress, and depression.

The following are common examples of cognitive distortions:

All-or-nothing thinking refers to adopting a dichotomous viewpoint in which there is never any place for uncertainty.

The act of picturing the worst possible outcome of an occurrence is known as "catastrophizing."

An example of overgeneralization is when one assumes that something will always be a particular way, even though there is only a limited amount of data to support that assumption.

The act of concluding something prior to having sufficient evidence to support that judgment, often known as "jumping to conclusions."

The belief that one may know what another person is thinking without the benefit of the required evidence is known as mind reading.

Signs that a person has been thinking too much, also known as overthinking, in the body.

Irritability is one of the symptoms of excessive overthinking that can be brought on by worrying and stress in excess.

2. Exhaustion.

3. having difficulty concentrating or remembering information.

4. Insomnia or other Sleep Disorders

5. Issues with the digestive system

6. Tension in the shoulders and the neck.

Every one of us, at some point or another, will find ourselves preoccupied with a single thought or concern. Finding out what triggers an issue is the first thing that needs to be done in order to fix it.

Among the signs that you might be ruminating or overthinking something are the following:

1. Spending a lot of time thinking about the same worries, problems, or anxieties over and over again

2. assuming the worst possible outcome by superimposing a detrimental occurrence from the past on the present and the future.

3. Having a persistent bad attitude about one's past or one's future for an extended period of time.

4. Letting your thoughts bring you down and causing you to feel disheartened or depressed.

5. Because you are preoccupied with one item in particular, it is difficult for you to concentrate on anything else at the same time.

6. the practice of continuing to think about a problem after having developed answers that are viable.

7. Being unable to move on to the next important matter as a result of continually dwelling on the same topic.

Distinguishing between the mental state of stress and that of excessive thought.

If you're constantly worrying about things that haven't happened yet or ruminating on something that already has, it's likely that you're overthinking the situation. It's possible that you'll experience this way of thinking when you're anxious or upset. It is possible that you will start to ponder the following questions: "What will happen next?" and "Have I done enough to prepare for the upcoming event?"

Think about how you are currently feeling.

It is very normal to experience feelings of apprehension or fear from time to time, particularly when one is presented with novel challenges. If you discover that you are focused on these feelings an excessive amount, you may be overthinking the situation.

Strategies For Avoiding Or Putting An End To Excessive Or Unnecessary Pondering

Learning to stop acting on all of our thoughts and instead focusing our attention on the here and now is the only way to break the habit of overthinking. The following is each of the four steps:

1. Keep our attention on the task at hand throughout the day. It is imperative that we are constantly conscious of and mindful of the fact that excessive thought defeats the aim.

2. As soon as we become more conscious, we should initiate the practice of observing our thoughts. That is, anytime we find ourselves thinking, rather than acting on what we are thinking, simply observe how it is that

we are thinking. When we do this, it will immediately stop working properly.

3. We should only allow ourselves to think about something when it is absolutely necessary. For instance, when determining the daily tasks that are most important to us, we ought to give some thought before acting. It's possible that will take up to five minutes. During times like this, it is not only permissible but encouraged for us to think and act based on those views. In a similar vein, when we write in a journal, we are also thinking about what we are writing. That is an appropriate alternative as well. We are making an effort to cut down on the amount of time that is spent thinking. We have no interest in becoming monks.

4. Make the most out of this amazing life! It is imperative that we let go of all concerns regarding the past and the future. This is due to the fact that

tomorrow will never come, and the day before has already gone by! Appreciate the fact that we are here right now, regardless of how much we hope to accomplish in the future or how much we have struggled through in the past.

Medication and Non-Medical Treatments are Available.

Anxiety is a prevalent mental health condition that impacts the lives of millions of individuals all over the world. It can be debilitating, generating a persistent sense of anxiety and concern that interferes with day-to-day life and can make it difficult to function normally. A significant number of people who are afflicted with anxiety seek relief through the use of pharmaceuticals or non-traditional therapies.

Treatments for Anxiety with Medications

Medication is frequently recommended to assist in the management of the symptoms of anxiety. These drugs are effective because they regulate substances in the brain that are involved in emotional processing and mood. SSRIs, or selective serotonin reuptake inhibitors, and benzodiazepines are the types of drugs that are most commonly recommended to treat anxiety.

Categories and Important Considerations

In most cases, the initial treatment for anxiety is with a selective serotonin reuptake inhibitor (SSRI), such as Prozac or Zoloft. They are helpful in alleviating the symptoms, and in comparison to other drugs, they have fewer negative side effects. However, it could take many weeks before they begin to have their effect.

Benzodiazepines, which include Xanax and Klonopin, operate rapidly to alleviate the symptoms of anxiety, but their usage over an extended period of time can lead to addiction. They are normally only intended for use for a limited period of time or in the event of an anxiety attack.

It is crucial to have a conversation with your healthcare professional about the benefits and drawbacks of each type of medication. They will be able to assist you in determining the treatment that is most appropriate for your individual requirements and monitor any potential adverse effects.

Alternative Treatment Methods

Over the past few years, there has been a rise in both interest in and utilization of alternative therapies for the treatment of anxiety. These treatments take an integrated approach to addressing anxiety, focusing on the mind as well as the body. Herbal cures, acupuncture, as well as activities like yoga and tai chi, are examples of well-liked alternative treatments for anxiety.

Natural Cures and Remedies

Herbal remedies are medicines that are made from plants and have a long history of usage in traditional medicine. It is thought that both the mind and the body might benefit from their relaxing effects. Chamomile, lavender, kava, and passionflower are just few of the plants that are frequently used to treat anxiety. Herbal treatments are helpful for a lot of individuals, but you should be aware that they can have negative interactions with other kinds of medicines and that they aren't necessarily appropriate for everyone. Before attempting any herbal treatments on your own, it is in your best interest to speak with a qualified medical professional.

Treatment with acupuncture

Acupuncture is a traditional Chinese medicine technique that includes inserting very thin needles into certain places on the body in order to stimulate the body's natural healing processes and reduce the severity of various illnesses. It is thought to assist balance the flow of energy throughout the body, as well as alleviate tension and anxiety. Even though there is just a little amount of scientific data to support its effectiveness, a large number of people claim that acupuncture has helped them.

Yoga and Tai Chi

Yoga and tai chi are mind-body practices that combine physical movement with mindfulness techniques. They focus on deep breathing, stretching, and relaxation, which can help reduce stress and anxiety. Regular practice of these activities has been linked to improved mental well-being and reduced symptoms of anxiety. They are also low-impact and accessible for people of all fitness levels.

The Significance Of Having A High Level Of Emotional Intelligence

We have finally arrived to the most important chapter in this book. The idea that I am about to present to you is without a doubt going to be the most important one covered in this whole article. I am referring to the idea that is commonly referred to as "emotional intelligence." There is a good chance that you have encountered this concept in the past. In point of fact, you might have come across it on the internet or in a book that is conceptually comparable to this one. However, before we move on, I have a question for you: how accurate would your explanation of the concept of "emotional intelligence" be if someone asked you to provide one?

Your comprehension of emotional intelligence should reach a high level of precision by the time you've finished reading this chapter; that's my hope for you. You will be in a position to differentiate yourself from other individuals who have merely a surface-level understanding of such an essential topic as emotional intelligence if you have knowledge that is both detailed and exact. Additionally, the more theoretical information you have, the more adept you will be at applying what you know in practice. This is because you will have more theoretical knowledge. Theory and practice ought to always go hand in hand, in my opinion, and I am confident of this. For this reason, I have devoted parts of this article to theoretical understanding before going on to practical advice that you may apply to bring more calm and peace into your life.

The questions that are going to be covered in this chapter that are going to be the most important ones are going to be: which theory (or group of distinct theories) provides a satisfactory explanation of emotional intelligence? Why is it so vital to have a high degree of emotional intelligence if we want to be able to feel good about ourselves? And as a final question, is there a correlation between having high emotional intelligence and being successful in one's job? How can this connection be explained in a way that is crystal clear and unmistakable if the answer to the previous question is yes?

Continue reading if you want to learn everything there is to know about emotional intelligence!

Embracing The Strength That Comes From Motion

It is impossible to list all of the benefits that come with maintaining a consistent workout routine. A dynamic ally for persons who are battling anxiety and panic attacks, in addition to enhancing energy, elevating mood, and making it easier to get restful sleep, it also facilitates better overall sleep quality. The release of pent-up tension and the lessening of feelings of unease and dread can both be accomplished through the medium of engaging in physical activity.

A regular workout routine can help address multiple aspects of the difficulties that are caused by anxiety. To begin, it alleviates the physical stiffness that is frequently a symptom of anxiety, which functions as a natural cure for the condition. In addition, physical activity causes the release of endorphins, which are the body's natural elixirs of happiness and well-being. These powerful chemicals not only alleviate discomfort and stress, but they also reduce the body's susceptibility to anxious responses, which in turn lessens the intensity of panic attacks and the frequency with which they occur. In addition, engaging in regular physical activity helps to reduce the production of stress hormones, which in turn contributes to a heightened feeling of equilibrium.

Incorporating regular exercise into your routine is more than simply a physical challenge; it's also a form of self-care that you're doing for yourself. It's a decisive step toward overcoming anxiety and panic disorders, and it's a move in the right direction. You'll notice a discernible increase in self-assurance as you bask in the plethora of benefits that come from engaging in physical activity on a regular basis. This will propel you toward lower anxiety and improved overall health.

Reevaluating Your Nutritional Options is Covered in Chapter 5

Even though your eating habits may not directly cause anxiety in you, they can surely influence the severity of the condition if you are genetically predisposed to anxiety disorders. In recent years, an increasing number of studies have established correlations between the foods we eat and our mental health. It's possible for certain foods to be therapeutic, helping to boost your mood and relieve tension at the same time. On the other hand, some can make the symptoms much worse that you are trying to get rid of.

The relationship between eating and feeling anxious can be a powerful one. If you suffer from anxiety and panic attacks on a regular basis, it is in your best interest to examine the foods you eat and give some thought to making any required adjustments. To begin, stay away from foods that have the potential to exacerbate your anxiety:

- Foods that are Fried: These meals, which are notoriously difficult to digest and offer little in the way of nutritional content, can put a strain on the body and intensify its responses to stress.

- Alcohol: In addition to its ability to cause dehydration, alcohol disrupts nutritional and hormonal harmony, and the poisons that it contains have the potential to cause anxiety episodes.

- Caffeine-Rich Products: Caffeine is a stimulant that quickens the heart rate and can cause feelings that are similar to those experienced during an anxiety attack. Caffeine can be found in beverages such as coffee.

- Dairy Products: Although dairy products do not intrinsically cause harm, excessive consumption might cause a rise in adrenaline, which is a possible anxiety booster.

- Refined Sugars: These sugars, which may be found in a variety of sweets and beverages, can cause the body to become overstimulated, which can lead to a state that is conductive to anxiety.

• Foods That Produce Acid Certain foods, such as pickles, yogurt, eggs, wine, and liver, all have an acidic pH. Magnesium is a mineral that is intrinsically connected to anxiety responses, and some research suggests that eating such foods can reduce magnesium levels.

To be more specific, omitting these foods from the diet might help the body deal better with anxiety. However, reducing or eliminating the offending substance entirely might alleviate the symptoms. Reducing your consumption of these foods, particularly if they make up the majority of your diet, may provide noticeable relief from anxiety levels.

Self-Evaluation Activities To Help You Gain A Better Understanding Of Your Attachment Style

The first step toward developing healthier relationships is gaining an awareness of your own attachment style, which can be accomplished through the completion of self-assessment activities. You will be able to determine the patterns and behaviours that are characteristic of your attachment type with the assistance of these assignments that require contemplation and introspection.

A Questionnaire Concerning Attachment Styles: The Attachment Style Questionnaire is a typical questionnaire for use in the process of self-evaluation. In most cases, it is made up of a series of claims or hypothetical scenarios relating to various attachment patterns. You are to mark, on a scale, the degree to which you agree with each of the statements.

Through the use of the questionnaire, you will be placed into one of the following four primary attachment style categories: secure, anxious, avoidant, or disorganized. This quiz, which can provide a fundamental analysis of your attachment style, is easily accessible online and costs nothing to complete.

Journaling That Is Reflective The practice of keeping a journal that is reflective is a potent kind of self-evaluation. Make it a habit to sit down and write regularly about your thoughts, feelings, and the experiences you've had in your various relationships. Investigate times when you felt intense emotions, were in a disagreement, or were uncomfortable, and make an effort to recognize any reoccurring patterns or triggers. When you keep a reflective journal, you are able to obtain deeper insights on your attachment style because it forces you to observe your own behavior and emotional responses.

The Attachment Timeline: Create a timeline of your most significant romantic and non-romantic relationships from your past and place them in chronological order. It is important to keep a record of critical events, the dynamics of each relationship, and your reactions to them. Take note of any patterns that emerge in your experiences as well as any thoughts or events that keep coming up. Through the use of this graphic depiction, you will be able to recognize patterns that exist in your attachment style across a variety of relationships and situations.

The following is a letter that you should write to the younger version of yourself: Imagine writing a letter of compassion and understanding to your younger self, especially during the years when you were developing your character. Discuss each other's observations and encourage one another. Think about the ways in which your early interactions with your caregivers may have played a role in shaping the attachment pattern you have today. This practice can assist you in cultivating self-compassion and gaining insight into the factors that contribute to the formation of your attachment style.

Triggers from the Diary of Attachment: Maintain a journal that is focused only on the attachment triggers you experience. In the diary, jot down any events, occurrences, or interactions that trigger your attachment patterns. This could be anything from a circumstance to a conversation. Describe in detail your reactions, including your thoughts, feelings, and actions, in response to the trigger. As time passes, patterns and regular triggers will start to develop, and your grasp of your attachment type will grow as a result.

Attachment-type Interview: Discuss your attachment style in an open and honest manner with close friends, members of your family, or a therapist who is able to offer an objective point of view. Ask them for their thoughts on the things you do and the ways in which you interact with other people and the relationships you have. There are occasions when you could benefit from the insightful insights of others that you might not be aware of on your own.

Workbooks And Resources Focusing On The Attachment Style: Workbooks in the manner of attachments and other tools might be helpful while engaging in activities like self-evaluation and introspection. These tools usually include worksheets, activities, and other ways that you may use to conduct an in-depth investigation into your attachment type and how it affects the connections you have in your life.

Keep in mind that creating a comprehensive knowledge of your attachment style is a journey, and as you go through these self-evaluation tasks, be kind to yourself, curious about yourself, and self-compassionate as you go through the process. Remember that establishing a full understanding of your attachment style is a journey.

The ritual of starting the day with a steaming mug of coffee is something that many of us look forward to doing every morning. Caffeine, which can be found in beverages such as coffee, tea, soda, and energy drinks, is a psychostimulant that works by stimulating the central nervous system. It has been shown that taking it in low amounts can improve one's alertness, mood, and focus. However, consuming an excessive amount of caffeine might make anxiety and insomnia worse.

If you want to lower your anxiety levels, you should think carefully about the amount of coffee you consume and how it affects both your mind and your body. You can reset your tolerance to caffeine by abstaining from all forms of caffeine for a period of one month. This eliminates the jitters and provides you with a fresh start, allowing you to introduce back moderate amounts of caffeine in a conscious manner.

When you start reintroducing caffeine into your diet, you should stop drinking it by the early afternoon so that it can be eliminated from your system by evening. This eliminates the risk of sleep disruption, which is absolutely necessary for effective anxiety management. You can gradually reduce the amount of caffeine you consume by switching some of your coffees for decaf or herbal tea. Establish a clear limit in accordance with your own level of tolerance, which differs from person to person.

Pay attention to how the different amounts of caffeine affect your levels of energy and anxiety, as well as the quality of your sleep. Wean yourself off of medication carefully over the course of a few weeks to decrease the severity of withdrawal symptoms if you try going without but end up with severe headaches.

As an alternative to coffee when you need a pick-me-up in the afternoon, try drinking some herbal or green tea. Water should be your primary beverage of choice, so be sure to drink plenty of it.

Caffeine-containing pain medications, chocolate, and drink should be consumed in moderation.

By setting clear limits for how much caffeine you consume, you can avoid the drug from having power over you. Instead of allowing it to heighten your anxiety, learn to harness its power and use it wisely. You may still have pleasure in your cup of coffee in the morning without jeopardizing your capacity for inner calm if you practice mindful moderation.

Now, let's delve even deeper into the ways in which caffeine affects both the intellect and the body:

The Workings of Caffeine

• It inhibits the neurotransmitter known as adenosine, which is responsible for giving you a weary feeling.

• It peaks in your blood within 30-60 minutes and is removed from your system in 3-7 hours. • It increases the release of cortisol, adrenaline, and dopamine, which are "alertness" hormones. • It reaches its maximum concentration in your blood within those time frames.

Caffeine's Many Advantages

• When used in moderation, it improves alertness, reaction time, cognitive function, as well as mood.

• Improves athletic performance and endurance during workouts by providing antioxidants (from coffee and tea); • Provides these benefits.

Negative Effects of Consuming Too Much Caffeine

• Withdrawal from this substance is accompanied by jitteriness, headaches, and other symptoms.

• May make symptoms of anxiety, sleeplessness, and restlessness even more severe.

• When ingested in excess, it causes digestive troubles such as reflux illness and raises blood pressure and heart rate, which increases the chance of developing cardiovascular disease.

Tips for Maintaining a Moderate Caffeine Intake

- If you want to prevent having trouble falling or staying asleep, drink your final cup of coffee before 2:00 p.m.

- If quitting caffeine cold turkey is too difficult for you, try substituting decaf for your regular coffee.

- If you need a pick-me-up in the afternoon but want to avoid caffeine, try herbal teas like chamomile, turmeric, or mint. • Determine a limit for your personal tolerance, and stick to no more than one to two cups of coffee or tea each day.

- Choose more manageable serving sizes, such as 8-ounce cups, rather than large 20-ounce coffees.

- Choose lighter or medium roasts rather than darker ones because they contain less caffeine.

- As a healthier alternative to soda, try sparkling water spiked with lemon or lime instead.

Be on the lookout for these stealthy and covert sources of caffeine:

- There is a wide range of concentrations in chocolate, soft drinks, and energy beverages.

- Some non-cola sodas, such as Mountain Dew, have a caffeine content that is even higher than that of Coke.

- "Decaf" still includes 2-15 mg of caffeine per cup. • Pre-workout supplements and "fat burning" pills. • Excedrin and other over-the-counter pain medicines. • "Decaf" still contains caffeine.

You can still have pleasure in your morning cup of coffee without experiencing an increase in worry by practicing mindfulness. Pay attention to the cues your body sends you in order to locate the best zone of moderate caffeine consumption!

Instruction on Social Skills

Training in social skills is an important component in the process of overcoming social anxiety. Increasing your confidence and making it easier for you to interact in a variety of social contexts are both benefits of developing good social skills. If you want to be able to effectively manage social anxiety, honing these skills can make a major difference in your capacity to do so, whether you're dealing with interpersonal dynamics in the job, at social gatherings, or in your personal life.

1. Capabilities in Communication:

Successful social relationships are built on a foundation of clear and effective communication. You will be able to handle conversations with greater comfort and confidence if you work on developing your communication skills:

Active listening can be practiced by focusing one's entire attention on the person speaking, maintaining eye contact, nodding one's head occasionally, and asking questions that seek clarification. Not only will this help you engage in the conversation, but it will also demonstrate that you appreciate the person who is speaking.

Topics to Spark Conversation: Master the art of starting conversations by practicing with open-ended questions, praises, and sharing relevant tales with other people. Beginning a conversation with a new person might help ease the anxiety that comes with approaching strangers.

Learn different strategies for keeping the flow of a conversation going smoothly so that you can maintain it. This includes displaying empathy, delivering appropriate replies, and searching for areas of common ground.

2. Training in assertiveness The ability to be assertive is an essential skill for the management of social anxiety. It gives you the ability to effectively express your demands, boundaries, and opinions while also respecting the rights and boundaries of others:

Acquiring Knowledge of Assertiveness: Understand the distinctions between aggressiveness, passivity, and assertiveness. Finding a middle ground between being passive (which means avoiding conflict) and aggressive (which means neglecting the needs of others) is the goal of assertive communication.

How to Avoid Guilt When You Say "No" Many individuals who suffer from social anxiety find it difficult to say "no" when they are uncomfortable or overwhelmed. Training in assertiveness teaches people how to deny requests or invitations in a manner that is both courteous and aggressive.

Communicating What You Require: Get into the habit of articulating your ideas and emotions in a way that is unambiguous and forthright. This helps those around you comprehend your perspective and can lead to encounters that are more enjoyable overall.

3. Non-Verbal Communication: When it comes to social relationships, non-verbal cues play a very important role. You can exude confidence and interact with others in a more productive manner if you are skilled in nonverbal communication.

Body Language: It's important to be aware of your body language, which includes your posture, gestures, and facial expressions. Pay attention to all of these! The body language of someone who is confident exudes an air of openness and relaxation.

Eye Contact: Making the right kind of eye contact at the right time is an essential part of non-verbal communication. It shows that you are paying attention to the conversation and that you are interested in it.

Voice Quality Both the volume and the pitch of one's voice can be used to communicate a wide range of feelings. Exercise changing the tenor of your voice so that it fits the situation of the conversation.

4. Role-Playing and Simulation: Putting your social skills to the test in a controlled setting by participating in role-playing activities or social simulations is a great way to hone and improve your communication and interaction abilities. To participate in these activities, you could work with a therapist, sign up for a group that

teaches social skills, or even seek the assistance of a reliable friend or member of your family.

5. Desensitization through repeated exposure to the allergen:

The gradual introduction into social circumstances that cause one to experience anxiety is an essential component of social skills training. This method entails deliberately putting yourself in social situations that are progressively more difficult, which will help you build up your tolerance for anxiety:

Approach in a Step-by-Step Manner: You should begin with scenarios that are less likely to cause anxiety and progressively work your way up to those that are more difficult. As your self-assurance grows, you'll be able to take on increasingly difficult societal responsibilities.

The Value of Continual Effort and Practice: The more you engage in social interactions, the more proficient and at ease you will become in certain situations. The terror that is linked with particular circumstances can be diminished through repeated exposure to those circumstances.

Training one's social skills is an ongoing process that calls for patience and perseverance on the trainee's part. Keep in mind that making mistakes is an inevitable component of the educational process, and that every contact presents a chance for personal development. You can build strong social skills that enable you to handle social anxiety and engage comfortably in a variety of social contexts with time and constant effort. These skills will allow you to develop them.

Embracing Your Own Needs And Caring For Yourself

Imagine that you are on a significant journey through challenging periods such as feeling anxious or depressed. It seems as if you are traveling through a turbulent sea. But, what do you think? On this peaceful island, you'll find a place to stop and rest. This island is all about self-care and getting to a better place mentally and physically.

This chapter is similar to a map in that it will show you where to find unique things, such as a sense of well-being and tranquility. It's similar to how a skilled sailor may adjust the sails on their boat to ensure their safety when sailing through rough seas. If you take care of yourself, you'll be in a better position to learn how to deal with challenging circumstances when they arise in your life.

Consider how practicing self-care can serve as a practical guide that leads you to less stressful periods in your life. Imagine tending to a garden in your head instead of a physical one. You take care to ensure that the joyful and tranquil aspects of you continue to flourish. You are the captain of a relaxing ship dedicated to self-care. When things get difficult, there are many helpful things you can do to make yourself feel better and to maintain your strength.

But wait on there a second! Let's have a conversation about something significant before we go out on our trip. Even though taking a bath or lighting scented candles might be very relaxing, those aren't the only ways to practice self-care. It is more about doing little things on a daily basis that help you feel good and keep your attention on the here and now. You will be able to maintain command of your emotions, even when they are at their most intense.

Don't be concerned! To begin taking care of oneself, you do not need to have any prior experience or knowledge in the subject. You might think of us as friendly guides who will teach you how to take care of yourself and your needs. We will guide you through new and unfamiliar things, such as using a map with unique markers for happiness, kindness to oneself, and feeling internally balanced.

Imagine that practicing self-care is like having a bunch of supportive friends by your side, each of whom possesses a unique ability that can assist you on your journey. There is a buddy who can assist you in being calm and relaxed, and there is another friend who can alleviate stress by playing music that is calming. Everyone in this circle of friends can contribute to helping you feel stronger and more in tune with yourself on the inside.

Practicing Regular Activities Can Provide Long-Term Relief From Anxiety

A Day-to-Day Approach to Long-Term AnxietyThe pursuit of a life free of tension and characterized by calmness should begin with the establishment of regular daily routines. Even though there is no known treatment for anxiety, incorporating certain behaviors into your daily routine can help to significantly reduce the impact that anxiety has on your life. In this chapter, we will take a look at four important daily routines that could lead to a reduction in anxiety over the long run.

The Effects That Sleep and Diet Have On One Another

Imagine that your mind and body together make up a well-oiled machine. In order for it to function correctly, it is necessary to provide it with the appropriate fuel and to do routine maintenance. A good night's sleep and a healthy diet are two of the most essential components of this upkeep.

It is common practice to grossly underestimate sleep's ability to affect our mental wellness. Anxiety can be made worse by not getting enough sleep, which can magnify even the smallest of challenges and make them feel insurmountable. Putting one's sleep needs first is not a luxury but rather a necessity. The quality of sleep can be improved by establishing a regular sleep pattern, creating a comfortable sleeping environment, and engaging in relaxing activities in the hours leading up to bedtime.

On the other hand, proper nutrition is absolutely necessary for maintaining consistent levels of both energy and mood. It's possible that the nutrients your body needs to function effectively can be obtained through eating a diet that's healthy, well-balanced, and full of whole foods. In addition, there is evidence that a number of nutrients, such as omega-3 fatty acids and B vitamins, are associated with improved mental health. It may also be helpful to cut back on coffee and sugar consumption, both of which have been shown to make anxiety symptoms worse.

The Connection Between Working Out and Experiencing Anxiety

The battle against anxiety might benefit greatly from regular physical activity. Endorphins are naturally occurring chemicals that have the effect of lifting your mood and are produced in your body as a result of physical activity. Participating in physical activity on a consistent basis has been shown to reduce overall levels of stress hormones and to enhance the production of chemicals that contribute to a sense of well-being in the body.

To obtain these benefits, becoming a fitness enthusiast is not necessary in any way. Walking, doing yoga or cycling are all examples of simple activities that may help relieve anxiety. Maintaining a consistent workout routine is quite important; try to complete at least 30 minutes of moderate physical exercise on most days of the week.

anxiety Reliever

Strategies For Avoiding Anxiety As A Preventive Measure

In order to lessen the possibility of acquiring anxiety disorders, preventative interventions for anxiety concentrate on eliminating the variables that put a person at risk and encouraging healthy ways of living.

Although it is not always feasible to completely avoid anxiety from occurring, the following measures can considerably minimize the likelihood of experiencing anxiety and increase general well-being:

1. Stress Management It is extremely important to acquire skills that are helpful in managing stress. Anxiety can be significantly exacerbated by prolonged exposure to stress. Individuals may find that engaging in stress management strategies such as meditation, yoga, or mindfulness can

assist them in coping with the pressures of daily life.

2. Participating in Regular Physical Activity Research has shown that engaging in regular physical activity can lower the risk of anxiety. Endorphins, which are natural "happy" chemicals, are the ones that are released when you exercise.

Additionally, it facilitates a more effective regulation of stress hormones within the body.

3. Eating a Nutritious and Balanced Diet: Consuming the necessary nutrients for optimal brain health can be obtained by eating a nutritious and balanced diet. Fish and nuts both contain omega-3 fatty acids, which have been associated to a reduced risk of developing anxiety. Keeping your intake of sweets and caffeine to a minimum will also assist in maintaining a stable mood.

4. Getting Enough Sleep Put getting enough sleep at the top of your priority

list and build a consistent routine for getting it. Because a disturbed night's sleep might make a person more prone to anxiety, it is crucial to get the amount of restorative sleep that your body needs.

5. Moderate Your Use of Alcohol and Other Drugs Be aware of your consumption of alcohol and other drugs. Using these substances to excess or developing a dependent on them can raise the risk of experiencing anxiety. Seek help as soon as possible if your use of substances is causing you concern.

6. good coping strategies It's important to start young with the instruction and practice of good coping mechanisms. Encourage honest conversation about feelings and offer help for constructively coping with sources of stress.

7. Strengthen Your Social Connections It is important to keep your social connections in good shape. Anxiety can be exacerbated by being alone for long periods of time. Develop a network of

family members and friends who can be there for you emotionally when things go rough and use that network to your advantage.

8. Time Management In order to alleviate thoughts of being overburdened, it is important to teach efficient time management skills. It is possible to reduce unnecessary stress by instructing people how to organize their duties and manage their time.

9. Consider Participating in Mindfulness and Resilience Training Programs You should think about participating in mindfulness and resilience training programs. These strategies assist people in building their mental and emotional toughness, which in turn makes them better able to deal with the difficulties of everyday life.

10. Seek treatment Early If You Notice indicators of worry in Yourself or Someone You Love If you notice indicators of worry in yourself or someone you love, seek treatment early.

Intervention at the appropriate time can stop anxiety from getting worse and prevent it from becoming more severe.

11. Positive Self-Talk: Encourage people to have positive conversations with themselves and have compassion for themselves. Instruct them how to question their negative thought habits and create a more positive and balanced mindset.

12. Education: Make sure you and those around you are well-informed about anxiety disorders. When people have a better understanding of the nature of their anxiety, the stigma associated with it can be reduced, and it will be much simpler for them to seek treatment when they require it.

13. Seek Professional Support If your anxiety symptoms do not improve or if they get worse, you should seek the assistance of a therapist or a psychiatrist. Anxiety can be prevented from becoming chronic and

incapacitating if it is diagnosed and treated at an early stage.

In a nutshell, preventing anxiety can be accomplished by lessening one's exposure to stress, embracing a healthy way of life, cultivating resiliency, and getting professional assistance when it's required. Individuals can lower their chance of acquiring anxiety disorders and have a life that is more balanced and rewarding if they put these tactics into practice on a daily basis and begin to promote mental well-being at an early age.

How to Use the Power of Positive Affirmations to Beat Sleep Anxiety and Find Serenity in Your Nights

Anxiety over falling asleep or staying asleep can be a trying experience that can leave you feeling agitated and exhausted. The use of positive affirmations, on the other hand, is a strong technique that you may use to overcome sleep anxiety and encourage a restful night's sleep for yourself.

In this chapter, we will discuss the notion of positive affirmations, go more into their advantages in relation to sleep anxiety, and present practical tips and examples for incorporating positive affirmations into your day-to-day life.

You may conquer sleep anxiety and have a restful night's sleep by creating a happy mindset and utilizing the power of affirmations.

Acquiring Knowledge of Positive Affirmations

A positive affirmation is a short, positive remark that is repeated to oneself in order to shift thoughts and beliefs towards a more positive and empowering mentality. Positive affirmations may be found in many different religions and cultures. These affirmations can be tailored to a variety of aspects of one's life, including the anxiety associated with sleeping. You can rewire your thought patterns and replace anxious or negative ideas with supportive and happy ones by intentionally selecting affirmations to repeat to yourself and then repeatedly saying those affirmations.

2 BEING AWARE OF THE FACTORS THAT MAY BE RESPONSIBLE FOR THE

DEVELOPMENT OF SOCIAL ANXIETY IN CHILDREN

Imagine going into a labyrinthine forest of psychological intricacies, where every turn reveals another layer of intricacy; this is what it is like for youngsters who suffer from social anxiety. In the following section, we will begin on an adventure that is analogous to exploring the depths of the ocean, with a focus on the world of social anxiety that exists in the minds of young people. We are going to meticulously explore the various threads that make up this tapestry. This will include the delicate dance that takes place between biology and environment, as well as the subtle interplay that occurs between heredity and upbringing. Our goal is to shed light on the murky areas and bring to the foreground the factors that contribute to the fact that certain children are more likely to struggle with social anxiety than others, despite the fact that both groups of children face similar social challenges.

The influence of one's genes

1. The Ancestry of the Family: According to some studies, having social anxiety may run in families, much like inheriting an old tea set from your grandmother. When a child's relative, be it a parent or sibling, struggles with social anxiety, it's as if the youngster has pulled a card from the hereditary deck that leans towards this anxious disposition. This can be the case even when the relative does not have social anxiety themselves. These genetic cards have the ability to reshuffle the deck of brain chemistry, which results in the child experiencing a one-of-a-kind symphony of neural responses whenever they are confronted with new social situations. It's almost as if genes are the conductors of a brain orchestra, choreographing how it sways and harmonizes in response to various environmental cues and influences.

2. Neurotransmitters, also known as Imagine the brain to be a busy chemistry lab, and serotonin to be the eccentric head researcher in charge of regulating mood and anxiety. However, here's

where things get interesting: just as different lab assistants each have their own one-of-a-kind idiosyncrasies, different genetic variations can fiddle with the way that these neurotransmitters function. It is the equivalent of having a group of creative scientists working in the laboratory, each of whom has their own set of blueprints. Some children may receive the genetic predisposition for high levels of anxiety from their parents, which can pave the way for disorders such as social anxiety to become the primary focus of their lives.

3. Temperament: The children's temperaments are dealt out at birth like a deck of cards, and some of them are assigned the "shyness" card. It's almost as if you're born with an inclination toward taking a mellower, more inward-looking attitude to the social scene of your existence. On the other hand, not every timid child develops social anxiety; it's more of a game of chance than anything else. But for individuals

who inherit both the "shyness" card and a genetic design favoring social anxiety, it is as if the chances are stacked against them in the game of social anxieties. Shyness is characterized by an extreme lack of confidence in social situations. This combination can be like adding extra spice to the recipe, making it more likely that they will cook up increased levels of social anxiety in themselves.

The Relationship That Exists Between One's Thinking, Feelings, And Actions

The Triangle of Thinking

Having a firm grasp on the cognitive triangle is like to being in possession of a road map to one's own psychology. This conceptual triangle links three essential aspects of your experience, namely your thoughts, feelings, and actions. Each vertex of this triangle is not simply present because it happens to be there; rather, it exerts an impact on the other two vertices and is itself subject to that influence.

At its most fundamental level, emotions are formed by thoughts. For instance, if you think to yourself, "I am going to fail," the feelings that may follow are worry and hopelessness respectively. In turn, behaviors are influenced by emotions. It is possible that your feelings of hopelessness will cause you to put off taking action, which will, in turn, have a negative impact on your performance. This is an example of a self-fulfilling prophecy.

However, it is not a street that only goes in one direction; the links go in both directions. Emotions have the power to shape our thoughts in the same way that our thoughts have the power to shape our emotions. When you're nervous, you could start thinking things like, "I can't handle this," which might then have an effect on your behavior, possibly leading you to avoid or flee the unpleasant circumstance. Similarly, behaviors are another component that feed back into this system. Your beliefs (such as "I am capable") and feelings (such as increased mood or reduced stress) can be influenced and changed by engaging in a constructive action such as exercise, which in turn can reinforce your thought patterns.

Because it may be applied to both self-regulation and change, the cognitive triangle emerges as an extraordinarily potent instrument in this respect. You can effect change in the two other parts of the triangle by intervening at any point along the triangle's path. For instance, consciously choosing to entertain an optimistic notion such as "I can do this" can lead to the experience of happy emotions, which can then lead to improved performance or improved coping strategies.

Consider the possibility that a presentation at work does not go as smoothly as expected. A negative belief such as "I messed up everything" can lead to feelings of shame as well as behaviors such as withdrawing from social situations. What if, though, we were to stop that train of thought and reframe it? "The presentation could have been better, but it's an opportunity for me to learn." This modification in thought can lead to feelings such as hope or curiosity, as well as behaviors such as seeking feedback for the sake of improvement, so completing the triangle in a manner that is more adaptable.

It is essential to have a solid understanding of the fact that there is no one entrance point in the triangle that is superior for intervention; rather, it is dependent on your own circumstances, level of self-awareness, and the abilities you've developed through methods such as CBT. Because they are typically less difficult to access and analyze than either feelings or behaviors, distorted or dysfunctional thoughts are frequently the focus of therapeutic work. However, interventions can also be behaviorally driven, such as exposure activities for the treatment of anxiety disorders. These tasks then loop back to alter thoughts and feelings.

Having an understanding of the cognitive triangle provides us with a holistic perspective through which we may interpret, comprehend, and, ultimately, influence the experience of living our lives. In the next chapters, we will look into several real-world situations and different approaches to making decisions that are centeredaround this fundamental idea.

Recognize Any And All Cognitive Fractionations

We have already examined a variety of thought patterns that have the potential to both impede our progress and leave us feeling worse. On the other hand, cognitive distortions are the ones that occur most frequently. Cognitive distortions are errors in thinking that cause us to have an incorrect perspective on life's circumstances. Thoughts like these are not only detrimental and counterproductive since they prevent us from achieving our objectives but also raise the risk that we will experience mental health conditions like anxiety and sadness. Cognitive distortions are extremely common given that all of us are prone to making reasoning errors on sometimes. The regularity of their occurrence is what makes them risky. If you are aware that you frequently engage in cognitive distortions, then you need to make an effort to change this pattern.

Catastrophizing, one of the most common types of cognitive distortion, is something that we've already talked about in Exercise 3 of Chapter 3 of this book. But it's also possible that you have what's known as all-or-nothing thinking, also known as a black-and-white mentality. This means that you only focus on the most positive or negative events, and you ignore any gray areas. As a result, you think that you are either the best at everything or that you are the worst at everything, that your life is either an absolute paradise or a horrible tragedy, and so on. The assumption that your emotions are an accurate reflection of reality is at the heart of what psychologists refer to as emotional reasoning. You believe that if you have a certain feeling, then it must be true since you can't help but feel that way. For instance, if you experience loneliness, it indicates that you are by yourself and that no one likes you. Reading other's minds is a terrible reflection on you since it shows that you believe you can understand what other people are thinking and that you are arrogant. It's possible that you think the person you're speaking with doesn't like you because they aren't paying attention to what you have to say. Overgeneralization is yet another type of cognitive distortion that is rather widespread. This occurs when an individual takes a single unfavorable experience and applies it to all scenarios. Just because one of your dates didn't go well, you can start to believe that nobody likes you. The act of assigning a negative label to oneself or another person in such a way that prevents one from seeing them or themselves in any other light is known as labeling. It's possible that you think you're incapable, or that your closest buddy is an idiot. Even if there is evidence that runs counter to your beliefs, you will continue to believe that you are inept and that they are dimwitted.

The cognitive distortion known as fortune-telling causes an individual to believe that they are doomed, and that their future will be dismal regardless of the actions they take. In other words, you continue to assert that the results of all of your acts will be unfavorable despite the lack of evidence to support such a claim. You might, for instance, believe that it doesn't make a difference how much you study because you'll never graduate on time no matter how hard you try. When something positive happens to you, but you don't believe it to be as essential as if it were a terrible thing, this is an example of discounting the positive, also known as minimization. Consider the following thoughts as examples of dismissing the positive: (1) you received a good grade only because you were lucky; (2) your first date went well because the other person was nice and didn't want to hurt your feelings; and (3) your first date went well because the other person wanted to avoid upsetting you. Thinking in imperatives, also known as shouldsand musts, is yet another form of cognitive distortion that is quite common. It indicates that you continue to give yourself advice on what you ought to or ought not to do, as well as what you must or must not do. In spite of the fact that it could be helpful in certain circumstances, using it in excess will only make your condition worse. It's possible that telling oneself what you ought to or have to do will make you feel more motivated, but only if you do it in specific situations and don't keep saying it to yourself over and over again. Keep in mind that you are well within your rights to relax, enjoy yourself, and make errors. When you take things personally or place blame on yourself for something that is beyond your control, you are engaging in the process of personalization. It's possible that you think you're the reason of your parents' frequent arguments, or that people who make general considerations are actually referring to you. The mental filter, also known as selective abstraction, is the third and last category of cognitive distortion. It happens when you concentrate on the bad aspects of something and either forget about them or don't give the good or neutral aspects enough importance. Because of our tendency to remember the negative experiences more vividly than the positive ones, this is a mistake that each of us is guilty of making. Even if someone loves us and is really kind to us, we could choose not to accept them as a friend or partner because of only one mistake they did in the past.

In general, all of the cognitive distortions described above cause you to concentrate on the negative elements of your life rather than the positive aspects of your life. They force you to squander valuable resources, such as time and energy, which you could otherwise put toward achieving your objectives. If you find that you frequently give in to cognitive distortions, you can use the following three exercises to train yourself to notice and counteract those distortions.

Cbt Methods For The Treatment Of Anxiety

Now, let's speak about some practical approaches that you can employ from the field of cognitive behavioral therapy (CBT) to combat anxiety:

1. Recognizing Unhealthy ideas The first thing you need to do is become aware of when worrisome ideas enter your head. Put them in writing and keep them in a journal. This assists you in becoming more aware of the factors that cause your worry.

2. Calling Negative Thoughts Into Question Whenever you find yourself having a negative thinking, the first thing you should do is ask yourself whether it is founded on facts or fears. Evidence should be used to refute these views. Are your concerns grounded in reality?

3. Reframe Your Thoughts Once you have recognized unhelpful thoughts, you should make an effort to replace them with ones that are more positive or more balanced. If you find yourself thinking things like, "I'll definitely fail," try reframing such thoughts to say something like, "I'll do my best, and that's all I can ask of myself."

4. Gradual Exposure: Cognitive behavioral therapy may assist you to face your fear gradually if you are nervous about a specific situation, such as giving a speech in front of an audience. You should begin with steps that are easier to manage and gradually increase in size.

Consider the following scenario: you have a severe phobia of dogs. It is not necessary to begin by embracing a large and intimidating dog. Start by looking at photos of dogs, then go on to observing real dogs from a distance, and then work your way up to getting up close and personal with friendly and well-behaved canines. This method of slowing down helps to alleviate anxiety.

Training your brain to think differently and develop stronger coping mechanisms for anxiety is what cognitive behavioral therapy (CBT) is all about. This is a straightforward method that can be picked up by anyone. You can cultivate a stronger, more optimistic mindset and minimize anxiety's grip on your life by identifying and addressing negative thoughts as well as making use of these tactics.

Activities Performed On A Daily Basis That Contribute To The Preservation Of Mental And Emotional Health

When it comes to achieving long-term mental and emotional wellness, consistency is absolutely necessary. This chapter goes into the day-to-day activities that can help one maintain inner calm, composure, and resiliency. You may improve your mental and emotional health by making reading scripture, praying, and practicing self-care an integral part of your daily routine.

Including Readings from the Bible and Personal Prayer in Your Daily Routine

1. Take some time first thing in the morning to pray and contemplate so that you can get the most out of your day. Pick a verse from the Bible that speaks to you, and then spend some time in reflective silence thinking about what it

means. Make a prayer to God asking for direction and strength for the day ahead.

Prayer Example: "Heavenly Father, as I begin this day, I seek your wisdom and grace. Thank you for being my guide." I pray that your words will be a lamp to my feet and a light to guide me on my journey.

2. Keeping a Scripture Journal: This involves keeping a journal in which you jot down passages of scripture that encourage and uplift you. Consider the significance they hold in your life and how they are connected to your mental and emotional health.

3. Stop for a Moment in the Middle of the Day: During the middle of your day, stop for a moment to connect with the Divine. Offer a prayer of thanksgiving for the blessings of the day and ask for direction in navigating any difficulties that may arise.

An example prayer is "Lord, in the midst of this busy day, I pause to thank you for your presence and ask for strength to face whatever comes my way."

4. Evening Meditation: Before going to bed, take some time to read a passage from the Bible or to pray and ponder on a verse. Take some time to ponder the happenings of the day and look for solace in the awareness that God is always with you.

A sample prayer could go something like this: "Generous God, as I lay down to rest, I entrust my cares to you." Your tranquility envelops me, and I put my faith in your ever-vigilant care.

Improving One's Social Skills: A Roadmap To One's Own Personal And Professional Development

It is impossible to stress how important it is to have strong social skills in a society that is becoming increasingly interconnected. These abilities are the key to establishing meaningful relationships, being successful in one's professional sphere, and deftly navigating the complexity of a variety of social settings. In this extensive chapter, we will begin on a trip to study practical ideas and approaches for increasing your social skills, so providing you with the ability to interact with confidence and connect with others in an authentic manner.

The Importance of Having Good Social Skills

The term "social skills" refers to a broad range of competencies that enable individuals to interact successfully with other people in a variety of contexts, including both personal and professional spheres of existence. It is vital to have an understanding of their tremendous significance:

Developing Personal Connections: A solid foundation for genuine interactions with one's friends, coworkers, and romantic partners is a set of social skills that is rock solid. These qualities provide the foundation for long-lasting and meaningful connections with others.

Success in a Career: In the world of work, the capacity to communicate convincingly, collaborate fluidly, and network effectively is frequently the deciding factor in determining who will rise above mediocrity and into excellence. The path to achieving one's professional goals is through the cultivation of one's social abilities.

The resolution of conflicts: Life is full with arguments, disagreements, and opportunities for negotiation. Individuals who are equipped with effective social skills are able to handle these hurdles with elegance, so transforming potential friction into productive discourse and compromise.

Personal Development: The process of improving one's social skills is inextricably linked to one's overall growth as an individual. It is beneficial to one's self-esteem, it lessens the effects of social anxiety, and it promotes a greater understanding of both oneself and others.

Components Crucial to the Development of Better Social Skills

1. Being Aware of Oneself: Your road toward greater social skills should begin with the cultivation of increased self-awareness. Engage in some self-reflection and think back on your past experiences with other people so you can pinpoint areas in which you could

improve. The first step toward effecting substantial change in one's life is to develop a strong sense of self-awareness.

2. Engaging in Active Listening: Active listening is the foundation of effective communication. Train yourself to be totally present in discussions and to give the person who is speaking your complete and undivided attention. Avoid the temptation to interrupt and make sure your comments demonstrate empathy at all times. One way to promote conversation is to ask open-ended questions.

3. Communication That Is Not Verbal: The gestures, body language, facial expressions, and tone of voice that people use can convey a great deal of information. Pay careful attention to the non-verbal signs that you give off yourself, and work on developing the capacity to read and respond appropriately to the non-verbal cues that others give off as well.

4. Empathy: The capacity to comprehend and share the feelings of others is the hallmark of a profoundly connected human being. Empathy is the cornerstone of genuine human connection. Develop your capacity for empathy by making a concerted effort to examine circumstances from a variety of angles. This ability strengthens both your ability to connect on a deeper level and to create rapport with others.

5. Being Assertive: Striking a Balance Between Passive and Aggressive Communication It is an art to strike a balance between passive and aggressive communication. The communication of your views, feelings, and demands in a manner that is honest and courteous is an essential part of assertiveness. It gives you the ability to establish limits and speak for yourself in a way that is assertive without being aggressive.

6. Methods for Resolving Conflict: Conflict is an inescapable component of all social relationships. Finding solutions and common ground that are helpful to

both parties is the primary objective of learning skills for constructive conflict resolution. It avoids the pointless strategy of avoidance or escalation and instead focuses on creating beneficial outcomes.

7. Social Etiquette In order to successfully navigate the complex web of social relationships, it is essential to comprehend and abide by the social norms and etiquette that are in place. Spend some time getting to know the cultural norms and the expectations of different social settings so that you can adapt appropriately.

8. Mastering the art of small talk can substantially ease social encounters, particularly in new settings. This is especially true if you have mastered the art of small chat. Put some work into learning how to start conversations and being skilled at engaging in banter that is lighthearted and welcoming.

A Struggle Against Anxiety Through Acceptance and Meditation

I understand that the whimpers of worry may often turn into debilitating roars when we let them fester in the shadowy recesses of our brains, where feelings of dread continue to remain. It's like a raging storm that's going on in the background, whipping up anxieties, fears, and concerns, and making the whole world appear intimidating. But, dear reader, as you travel through the pages of this book, I want you to sense a reassuring presence, a gentle reminder that you are not walking alone through this storm. I want you to know that you are not in this storm by yourself.

At certain points in our life, each and every one of us will be accompanied by the invisible friend known as anxiety. It is an emotion that is shared by all people, a natural response to the symphony of our existence, and a reaction to things that are unknown and unexpected. It's the fluttering in your chest and the quickening of your breath when you're confronted with the unexpected; it's the darkness thrown by the unpredictability of the future.

When one is dealing with anxiety, it can frequently feel like they are traveling alone through a thick and dark forest. Nevertheless, it is essential to keep in mind that the light of camaraderie can shine through even the densest of canopies. Anxiety is the collective response that all of us have to the pressures and threats that exist in the world; it's a road that all of us take at some point in our lives, a common thread that is sewn into the fabric of our common humanity.

However, for some people, particularly us women, this shadow can develop and become a continuous, unwelcome companion, murmuring anxieties nonstop, casting a shade over the joys of the present, and creating a barrier to the straightforward pleasures of life. The sudden and powerful storms of panic attacks, the lingering fog of generalized anxiety disorder, or the specific and acute anxieties known as phobias are all examples of the many different manifestations that it is capable of taking, each with its own face and voice. Although every variety of anxiety has its own distinct dance, rhythm, and treatment, they all share the ability to cast long shadows over our thoughts and bodies.

As women, we frequently discover that we are dancing to the songs of additional societal and internal symphonies. These symphonies include the melodies of societal expectations, the rhythms of gender roles, and the harmonies of hormone shifts. In order to achieve harmony and balance, it is essential to recognize and comprehend these other layers that make up our music.

The process of overcoming anxiety can be challenging, but there are beacons of hope along the path in the shape of a variety of treatments and approaches that can be utilized along the route. One such lighthouse is the practice of mindfulness meditation, which entails a tender acceptance of the here and now as well as a compassionate, non-judgmental acknowledgment of each and every thought and feeling. It has been demonstrated that this method can calm an anxious mind, ease the physical manifestations of stress, and offer a sense of warmth to the spirit.

Breaking free from the shackles of anxiety is not an unattainable fantasy but rather a reality that is within reach if one has the right people, tools, and lighting to help them along the journey. Therefore, let's take a nice, slow breath together to calm ourselves down, and keep in mind that the ability to move gracefully through life and create our own song is already within each of us.

This book will take you on a journey through the many different landscapes of anxiety, where you will discover the many different faces of anxiety, comprehend the whispers it gives you, and learn how to dance in harmony through the practice of mindfulness meditation. It is my most sincere wish that the words contained within these pages will be your constant companion, assisting you in developing a healthier relationship with your own thoughts and feelings, leading you to the light that lies beyond the darkness, and assisting you in embracing a life that is full of splendor and satisfaction.

Let's go on this journey together, hand in hand, taking one step at a time, so that we can discover the depths of our brains and locate the path that will lead us to a life that is peaceful, well-balanced, and full of happiness. The road you are about to embark on is one of coming to understand, accepting, and love oneself; it is a journey toward embracing calmness.

The first chapter.

What exactly is a disorder of anxiety?

Have you ever stopped to think about why you were shaking before your test or why your palms were sweating before your job interview?

These jittery feelings are a perfectly natural way for the body to be ready for a significant event by preparing itself in advance.

You would have also noticed that as the event got underway, you began to relax down; you started to breathe better, and your heart stopped beating as quickly as it had been.

Because it makes us more conscious, this worry actually improves our performance at work.

Nevertheless, there are people who experience worry or periods of anxiety for no discernible reason. It's possible that you have an anxiety disorder if you struggle to keep your worries in check and if the persistent feelings of unease make it difficult for you to carry out the tasks of daily life.

What distinguishes normal anxiety from an anxiety disorder is the severity of the symptoms.

You can use this quick checklist to determine whether or not you have an anxiety problem by considering the following items:

A constant state of unease

Worrying about things like one's finances, upcoming job interviews or tests, or other significant upcoming events.

The feeling of having "butterflies in your stomach" before giving a speech in front of a large audience or participating in a major conference.

A fear of something that could potentially cause harm, such as a stray dog that barks at you when you're walking down the street.

Concern or melancholy experienced in the immediate aftermath of a traumatic event, such as the loss of a loved one.

Keeping both yourself and your immediate environment clean is very important.

Starting to perspire just before a very important competition.

Disorders related to anxiety

When you worry constantly and excessively for no apparent reason, it makes it more difficult for you to complete the activities of daily living.

Having a fear of participating in any activity, be it social or performance-related, that can put you in the position of being judged or criticized by other people.

You are concerned that you will act in a manner that will bring shame or embarrassment to yourself or others.

An irrational fear of a thing or place, such as the anxiety that comes from entering an elevator because of the false belief that there is no way out.

After being exposed to an extremely traumatic event in the past, the individual may experience recurring flashbacks, nightmares, and subsequent distress.

What are the factors that lead to anxiety disorders?

The following are the most common contributing factors that lead to anxiety disorders:

People who come from families where there is a history of mental health issues are more likely to struggle with anxiety than those who do not come from such families.

For example, OCD may be passed on from generation to generation in a family.

Events that are stressful, such as having a stressful job, dealing with the death of a loved one, or having challenging relationships, may also generate feelings of anxiety.

Health problems: Conditions such as thyroid problems, asthma, diabetes, or heart disease can all contribute to an increase in anxious feelings. It's possible for people who are depressed to also start exhibiting indicators of anxiety disorders.

For example, a person who has been suffering from depression for a significant amount of time may begin to underperform at their place of employment.

This could then result in stress related to work, which could contribute to feelings of worry.

People who are strong users of drugs, alcohol, or other substances may struggle with anxiety as the effects of the substance begin to wear off (this process is known as withdrawal).

A person's personality may have a role in their susceptibility to anxiety-related diseases. For example, people who strive for perfection or who have a strong desire to take the lead may be more likely to suffer from these conditions.

Investigating How Attention Deficit Hyperactivity Disorder Can Affect Intimacy And Relationship Bonding

It is essential for couples who live with ADHD (attention deficit hyperactivity disorder) to get an understanding of how the illness can impact feelings of intimacy and the bonds that form within relationships. ADHD has a wide-ranging impact on a person's life, including the ways in which they are able to connect with their spouse emotionally, intellectually, and sexually.

In this section, we will delve into the complex ways in which ADHD affects the intimacy and relationship relationships between people, shedding light on the challenges, and providing insights into how to handle them.

1. The Connection Between Emotional Intimacy and ADHD

Emotional connection serves as the foundation for a healthy and fulfilling romantic partnership. On the other hand, ADHD can present its own set of challenges when it comes to forming and sustaining emotional connections.

Impact on the Ability to Form Emotional Connections: - Impulsivity and Emotional Reactions: People who have ADHD may have heightened impulses, which can lead to quick emotional reactions that might strain emotional connection. This can be a challenge for individuals who are emotionally connected to one another. It may be difficult for the partner to understand or cope with these abrupt shifts in mood.

- Difficulty in Expressing Emotions: Attention Deficit Hyperactivity Disorder (ADHD) can impair a person's capacity to adequately describe and communicate their feelings. It is more difficult to put one's sentiments and thoughts into words, which limits the degree of emotional proximity that can be achieved.

- Difficulty Maintaining Attention During Crucial Emotional Conversations Individuals who have ADHD may have difficulty maintaining attention during crucial emotional conversations. Because of this lack of attention, the partner may have feelings of being neglected or rejected, which is detrimental to the emotional relationships.

The Handling of Anxiety

You have a lot of options available to you to help you deal with anxiety on a day-to-day basis. One option is to prioritize taking care of oneself. This includes getting a enough amount of sleep, eating a healthy diet, engaging in physical activity, and participating in activities that you find enjoyable. In addition to this, it is essential to establish limits and prioritize your own needs. It is OK, for instance, to decline more commitments when you already have too much on your plate.

Learning to recognize and deal with the things that set off your anxiety is another essential component of anxiety management. The circumstances, individuals, or things that can bring on emotions of anxiety are referred to as triggers. When you've pinpointed the factors that set off your anxiety, the next step is to devise ways to manage the effects of those triggers. Exercising deep breathing, practicing grounding skills, and having pleasant conversations with oneself are all examples of coping tactics.

It is vitally crucial to pay attention to your ideas in addition to mastering the skills necessary to control your triggers. Cognitive distortions, often known as negative thought processes, are a potential contributor to increased anxiety. Catastrophizing, thinking in black-and-white categories, and leaping to conclusions are a few instances of cognitive distortions. It can be highly advantageous to learn to notice these distortions and reframe your thinking after you've identified them.

Last but not least, let's discuss how essential it is to take care of both your mental and physical health. Headaches, muscle tightness, and stomachaches are common examples of the kinds of physical symptoms that can be brought on by anxiety. Relaxation techniques are among the most effective methods available for reducing the physiological effects of anxiety. These include a systematic approach to muscle relaxation, deep breathing, and meditation on the present moment.

Applications That Push the Boundaries of Mindfulness

In recent years, creative ways have broadened the use of mindfulness in anxiety management, including the following:

1. Digital Mindfulness applications: With the advancement of technology came the creation of digital mindfulness applications. These apps provide guided meditation sessions, mindfulness activities, and tracking tools. The availability of these apps makes mindfulness more approachable, hence enabling users to incorporate it into their day-to-day activities.

2. Virtual Reality (VR): The technology behind VR allows for experiences that are completely immersive. Inside of a computer-generated world, users have the opportunity to wander among serene settings and take part in guided

meditation. The practice of mindfulness in virtual reality can help to improve relaxation and lower anxiety.

3. Integration of Biofeedback Devices Mindfulness techniques can incorporate biofeedback devices, which assess physiological responses such as heart rate variability and skin conductance. Users are provided with real-time feedback on their levels of stress, which enables them to better customize their mindfulness practices.

4. Mindful Gaming: The gamified versions of mindfulness apps and video games blend fun and relaxation. These games frequently include exercises in mindfulness, and they encourage players to make mindfulness a regular part of their life by including it in the games itself.

5. The Practice of Mindfulness in Educational Settings Students can learn how to manage stress and their emotions via the use of mindfulness programs that have been implemented

in educational settings. The results of some recent studies suggest that practicing mindfulness can lessen the effects of anxiety and boost academic performance.

Letting Go Of Mental Attachments AndDetachements In Order To Release Them

The following are five effective methods for releasing emotional attachments: Put an end to your antiquated ways of thinking.

Do you understand that it's possible that you still use the same mental processes you did when you were a child? That is absolutely correct. At birth, our genes and the environment both contribute to the programming that occurs in our brains. In order to free yourself from an attachment, you must first eliminate your previous thought. When it comes to letting go of long-held ideas and patterns of behavior, you may find it helpful to collaborate with a trained professional. Because I regularly find myself returning to old, unhelpful thought patterns, the first step for me was to figure out what those patterns were and how to overcome them.

Determine the Value You Place on Yourself:

Developing a healthy sense of self-worth can be an effective method for the healing of emotional scars. You can learn to let go of control by assisting yourself with techniques such as daily affirmations and mantras. I am capable is a powerful mantra to tell yourself, among other powerful mantras.

I take pleasure in challenges, as well as the education I receive from prevailing over them.

Every day, I make strides toward becoming a better person in every facet of my life.

There are beliefs about oneself that you hold unconsciously. The fact that there is negativity in the world is often hidden from our view. You may conquer negative thoughts by focusing on positive concepts and employing mantras that you repeat over and over.

Learn More About Your Real Self

Insecurities regarding our identities can occasionally give rise to emotional difficulties in our relationships. Do you have any idea what your interests and passions are? What kinds of things pique your interest? Finding out what drives you might be a helpful step toward overcoming emotional attachments to the people and things in your life. If you are having trouble figuring out who you are, you might ask other people to do the work of defining you for you so that you can focus on finding out who you are. On the other hand, doing so can result in codependency and make it impossible, in the long run, to free oneself from harmful emotional relationships.

Your perceptions are what shape the world around you.

To break free from those attachments, you will need to do certain actions. Learn to identify your feelings and locate the part of your body where they are stored. Maybe you eat when you're upset or participate in other behaviors that are harmful to yourself. After grasping and readjusting your consciousness to the challenges you are facing, you can direct your attention toward the pursuit of finding healthier solutions that will facilitate your transition into a more positive and robust condition. For instance, a person who eats when they are feeling upset might reason that if they devote themselves entirely to meditation and other physical practices, it will help them overcome the need to eat when they are feeling emotional.

Make Room For Both Practice And Forgiveness

Keeping one's grip on the past is extremely detrimental. Despite the fact that this may be the obstacle that is the most challenging to overcome for some people, it is nevertheless important to point out. Forgiveness means making peace with the past while maintaining an openness to new experiences and opportunities. Only you can forgive yourself; no one else can benefit from it. Developing emotional attachments is a common consequence of clinging to negative emotions such as rage and despair. Letting old wounds heal makes room for new lessons to be learnt, thus it's important to do both. After you have let go of these attachments and learned to forgive, you will at long last be able to go on.

Exercises that Help One Let Go and Move On

Several different practices will be able to assist us in severing these attachments:

1. Meditation: The practice of meditation consists of doing nothing more than sitting quietly and trying to concentrate on the here and now, be it your breath, your body, or the world around you.

You'll become aware that your focus wanders away from the present moment and becomes distracted with worries about the future, making plans, and remembering things that happened in the past. During meditation, you practice letting go of these minor attachments by first becoming aware of what your mind is doing and then letting go and returning your attention to the here and now. As a result of this happening regularly, you will get skilled at it. After hundreds of millions of repetitions, it feels almost exactly like using muscle memory. You come to the conclusion that whatever it was that you had become emotionally attached to was nothing more than a story, a narrative, or a fantasy. It's little more than a speck of cloud that can be dispersed by the slightest breeze.

2. Compassion: Through this meditation, you have the intention of putting an end to your own pain as well as the suffering of others. This wish shifts your focus from being unable to break free of your attachment to looking for a warm heart

that can help you break free of your attachment and find a solution to lessen the pain it causes. When you long for an end to your own suffering, you expand beyond the confines of your own story. And when you yearn for the end of the suffering that others are going through, you connect with them, acknowledge that your suffering is the same as theirs, and understand that you are all in this together. When you deal with people in this way, the significance of your attachments and the tale you've been telling becomes less important as time goes on.

3. the concept of interdependence. You might give some thought to concentrating not only on the wish that others' (and your own) suffering would disappear, but also on the wish that others might experience joy. Everyone else, regardless of whether or not you like them. Again, by doing so, you begin to see how you are all connected in the suffering that you experience and in the desire that you have to be happy. You are not as far apart from them as you would think. You cannot be separated but are, rather, depending on one another. Because of this connection with other people, you are able to feel less attuned to your physical surroundings and more at ease with life.

4. Letting Go and Accepting What Is An essential component of attachment is a fundamental lack of contentment with the present state of affairs. You are looking for an original solution. The reason for this is because there is something about the current circumstance, the person in front of you, or oneself that you do not like. You can start to trust that everything is fine just the way it is by meditating, practicing compassion, and developing an awareness of your interconnectedness with others. Although they are not "ideal," one may say that they meet the requirements. Even in its beauty. And as you start

to become more conscious of your persistent denial of the present moment, you also start to become more receptive to the realities of the here and now. This is the discipline, repeatedly opening oneself to the present moment, analyzing it with interest, and accepting it in its current state.

5. Capacity for expansion. All of these activities lead to a mind that is more open, one that is not so narrowly focused on its own tiny story of how things should be, one that is not so narrowly focused on its own small desires and aversions, but can view those as part of a wider picture. All of these practices result in a mind that is more expansive. These relatively little desires, along with a great number of others, can be filed away in the mind. It is a vast open space, comparable to a vast ocean or a beautiful blue sky, and the insignificant attachments are merely a part of it. However, it is also able to see the suffering of others and their attachments, as well as the present moment in all of its flaws and glory, and it is able to be present with all of this at the same time. At the moment, the practice is somewhat pricey.

Respect for Oneself

The low self-esteem and lack of confidence that an anxiety sufferer experiences on a daily basis is maybe the most significant aspect of the condition. To guarantee that you are effectively combating your anxiety, you should first work on boosting your confidence and improving your sense of self-worth. Nick overcame his anxiety and was able to finally break free from the hold that his anxiety had on him as a result of this, which is maybe one of the most important elements in how he overcame his anxiety.

accomplish you ever find yourself thinking, "Oh no, I won't be able to do that"? Or you may say, "I can't go there because I'm simply not strong enough." These are the phrases that people who are similar to yourself utter over and over again. Get rid of these beliefs and proverbs and replace them with ones that are the complete opposite. This is what you need to accomplish. Try replacing phrases like "I can't do this!"

with "I can do this, bring it on!" when you find yourself in a challenging situation. When you say nasty things to yourself or have negative thoughts about yourself, you are putting seeds of doubt and negativity in your brain's subconscious. If you plant more seeds, then more trees of uncertainty will sprout in their place.

It is imperative that, rather than growing trees of uncertainty, one plants trees of positivity, self-assurance, and bravery. You have to fight anxiety every day, and every day you get up and do the same thing over and over again in the vain hope that anything would change. You may know this condition as anxiousness, but do you also know another name for it? It's known as having bravery! the bravery to continue doing what you do each and every day, despite the fact that other people are able to go about their lives without the challenges that you face. Even though you may not be aware of it just yet, you already possess the strength and willpower necessary to triumph over the adversary you are up against; the only difference is that you are currently oblivious to this fact.

Start acknowledging the fact that you do have the ability to prevail. Understand that what you are going through right now is a stepping stone on the path to a stronger version of yourself. Nick went through a specific train of thinking and uttered some things aloud prior to entering a circumstance that he knew would cause him to experience anxiety, which was walking outside. He started by shutting his eyes and putting himself into the role of a player in a video game. He pictured a floating experience bar above his head, and each time he faced his anxiety front-on and moved beyond of his comfort zone, the bar on the experience bar above his head filled up. Because the more challenging challenges you overcome, the more resilient you become. You end up being a better version of yourself. Life is nothing more than a game in which all of us participate, and everyone of us is a different character.

After going through the motions of thinking, he then verbalized a couple of his thoughts to himself in the form of words. You are currently self-programming your mind into a new way of thinking, and you are also planting the seeds of confidence in yourself at the same time. It's not too dissimilar to the routine that a boxer or fighter would go through before a bout. It is such an effective method of building a sense of confidence inside oneself that it is almost unrivaled. The following is a list of phrases that have been shown to be effective when communicating with Nick and can be used by you:

"This is not going to be difficult at all."

"I've got this, there's no need for anxiety today!"

I am completely in charge of how I feel at all times.

"I'm incredible, and the rest of the day is going to be stress-free!"

"I'm a beast, and nothing is going to be able to stop me!"

"Anxiety is weak and I am strong," the person said.

"I am strong, powerful, and confident," was the statement.

"I'm not going to let anything stand in my way," she said.

The sentences presented here are examples of those that have been shown to be effective. It would be wonderful if you could come up with your own term that inspires confidence in yourself. Simply ensure that you say it three times while projecting confidence in order to begin the process of persuading yourself that you are who you are claiming to be. Now, let's look at a few things that you might say to yourself while you're experiencing a panic attack or are about to experience one.

"Is it the only thing that worries you?
"LET'S GET IT ON!"

"Whatever it is that I'm going through is going to go away at some point."

You're calling what I'm experiencing an anxiety attack? I've dealt with far worse!"

"Hahahaha, anxiety, go away I'm busy"
"Oh look, I have another anxiety attack coming, oh well...just hurry up and get on with it you stupid thing."

These sentences are stated with even more passion than the ones you say before heading into a scenario, which are similar to the things you say before going into a war. It's kind of like when you were a kid and your parents taught you to claim there are no monsters in the world even though you knew better. You keep repeating that phrase until you no longer have any fear of supernatural beings. The same is true for us now, except instead of getting rid of the monster in the closet, we are getting rid of our worry monsters. So while you are in the midst of a panic attack, focus on a specific statement such as "Whatever I'm experiencing is going to pass" and keep repeating it until the fear begins to subside. You will eventually arrive at the spot where it will go in a few seconds at most. What you are saying to yourself is not only a method of self-encouragement; it is also a method of anchoring for your stable emotions.

You will gradually find yourself saying things like, "Oh, I can't wait for today, let's see what the day brings!" if you consistently reinforce yourself with similar ideas and phrases throughout the day. Should Anxiety decide to make an appearance, I can't wait to show it who's in charge! As long as you follow the instructions, you should start to notice a significant increase in both your confidence and your self-esteem. Start regaining control of your self-confidence so that you can demonstrate to the world that YOU are the one in charge.

One strategy that cognitive behavioral therapy (CBT) employs to assist people overcome self-esteem problems is to encourage them to view the fundamental ideas with which they struggle as nothing more than views, which is exactly what these beliefs are. There is no evidence to support what you assert, despite the fact that you do. There is no indication that individuals hold a negative opinion of you. You might be surprised to learn that more people like you than you give yourself credit for.

These ideas continue to surface in your mind as thoughts and behaviors that are unfavorable to you. The more you dwell on them, the more your brain reconciles itself to the idea that they are the new standard. There are methods at your disposal that can be used to fight against this. You and your therapist can collaborate on the process of building a new set of behavior patterns for you to follow.

The purpose of this exercise is to demonstrate to you that the unfavorable views you hold about yourself are not supported by any evidence. It is for the purpose of providing you with a logical depiction of things in their actual state, not in the one in which you believe they should be. Therefore, cognitive behavioral therapy focuses on correcting erroneous thought patterns. Retraining your brain to see things in a way that is more functional and balanced is the goal of this process.

If someone does not pay attention to you, you can conclude that they do not value you to the extent that you require them to, which might lead you to believe that they are ignoring you. It's possible that you've even convinced yourself that you're not worthy of their attention. On the other hand, this could not be further from the truth. It's possible that they are merely concerned with other things. It's possible that they are having trouble with something that you are unaware of.

You don't need to jump to the conclusion that everything is hopeless; instead, you should take action, give them a call, and have a conversation with them. It can even come as a surprise to you to find out that they were having a terrible day, but that your call helped make things better for them. Your disposition will improve, and you will experience an increase in positive feelings about yourself, if you reach out to others. Through cognitive behavioral therapy (CBT), one attempts to retrain the brain to dislike the initial negative beliefs that one has about how one sees herself and to see things in a new light.

How to define inefficient time management, as well as the connection between time and stress.

It is absolutely necessary for people to have effective time management abilities in order to accomplish their objectives and enhance their general well-being. On the other hand, a lot of people have trouble managing their time well, which can result in stress and worry as well as a reduction in productivity. In this chapter, we will define ineffective time management, investigate the connection between time and stress, and present some practical techniques for resolving this widespread issue.

The definition of inefficient management of one's time

Ineffective time management is the inability to successfully manage one's own time in order to accomplish one's goals and objectives in a timely manner. It can present itself in a variety of ways, including the following:

The sin of procrastination: Procrastination is the act of putting off decisions or duties to a later time, typically until the very last minute. This behavior can result in increased stress and decreased productivity.

a failure to properly prioritize: If tasks are not prioritized, it is possible to miss deadlines and experience a drop in productivity as a result of spending time on less important activities.

Inability to delegate: Some individuals have trouble passing on responsibilities to other people, which can result in a sensation of being overburdened and overworked.

Inefficient use of time: Making inefficient use of time can lead to spending an excessive amount of time on low-priority tasks or becoming sidetracked by activities that are not linked to work.

The first step toward finding a solution to this issue is gaining an understanding of the factors that contribute to inefficient time management. Individuals are able to devise ways to directly address fundamental causes if they first recognize the causes themselves.

The link between time pressure and stress

A lack of effective management of one's time can lead to increased levels of stress, which, in turn, can have a negative impact on both one's physical and mental health. The relationship between time and stress is a complicated one that is influenced by a number of different circumstances, including the following:

Control that is only apparent: People who have the perception that they are in command of their time are less likely to experience stress than those who feel as though they are powerless and drowning in their responsibilities.

The amount of work that needs to be done can contribute to a rise in stress levels, particularly when combined with inefficient use of time.

Inadequate breaks The failure to take adequate breaks on a regular basis might result in exhaustion and a drop in output.

Negative thinking: Patterns of negative thinking, such as catastrophizing or overgeneralizing, can contribute to increased levels of stress and lead to decreased levels of productivity.

People can benefit from adopting approaches to improve their time management skills and experience reduced levels of stress if they recognize the connection between time and stress.

Understanding Anxiety Through Both Art And Science

Anxiety is a complex and fundamentally human sensation that lends itself to being interpreted in a variety of ways, including through artistic and scientific lenses. According to the findings of modern scientific research, anxiety is a normal reaction that has its origins in the course of our species' evolutionary history. It is an element of our body's alarm system that notifies us to potential risks, and in this context, it performs a protective purpose by urging us to react to danger by either "fighting" or "running away from" it. In order to gain an understanding of the science behind anxiety, one must delve into the intricate relationships between chemicals in the brain, neuronal pathways, and physiological responses that all play a role in its development. On the other side, one's worry can be seen as a type of art, most notably in the way that it is exhibited by that particular person. Anxiety can take on as many forms of expression as there are colors on an artist's palette, and some people channel their anxious feelings into the production of artwork, music, literature, or other forms of expression that are reflective of their internal turmoil. Mindfulness and meditation offer some people the opportunity to engage in a sort of spiritual practice that is analogous to the process of creating an original work of art.

Individuals not only need to learn how to control their anxiety, but also how to deal with the complexities that accompany it, in order to master the art of anxiety. It is about establishing individual tactics and resilience, as well as creating a personalized set of coping techniques, which may involve therapy, self-doubt, or requesting aid from people who are closest to them in their lives. Those who are afflicted with anxiety can find it helpful to assemble their own collection of coping mechanisms, much like a talented artist would carefully select their brushes and colors before beginning their work. In addition, the incorporation of both science and art into the process of comprehending anxiety highlights the importance of taking an all-encompassing approach to one's mental health. A thorough comprehension of the human experience is achievable if one combines scientific knowledge of the physiological reasons of anxiety with creative and artistic means of expressing, managing, and transcending it.

The Components of Excessive Thinking

The mental phenomena known as overthinking, which is often referred to as ruminating, is characterized by the persistent and, most of the time, fruitless study of various ideas, problems, or potential outcomes. The process of overthinking is generally set in motion by a trigger thought or event, such as a decision, a mistake from the past, an upcoming event, or any other mental disturbance. After a trigger has been set off, the overthinking process is characterized by a never-ending loop of recurrent thoughts, most of which are connected to the incident that set off the trigger. For instance, an overthinker may be triggered by a social contact, which may cause them to mentally replay the conversation, examine the words and actions of the other person, and contemplate how the other person reacted to the dialogue. This thought loop is recurrent and intrusive, and it is frequently accompanied by an inflated view of the potential repercussions that may result from the event that triggered it. This inclination to overthink things can have the effect of amplifying the emotional impact of the phenomenon.

The mental phenomena known as overthinking, which is often referred to as ruminating, is characterized by the persistent and, most of the time, fruitless study of various ideas, problems, or potential outcomes. The process of overthinking is generally set in motion by a trigger thought or event, such as a decision, a mistake from the past, an upcoming event, or any other mental disturbance. After a trigger has been set off, the overthinking process is characterized by a never-ending loop of recurrent thoughts, most of which are connected to the incident that set off the trigger. For instance, an overthinker may be triggered by a social contact, which may cause them to mentally replay the conversation, examine the words and actions of the other person, and contemplate how the other person reacted to the dialogue. This thought loop is recurrent and intrusive, and it is frequently accompanied by an inflated view of the potential repercussions that may result from the event that triggered it. This inclination to overthink things can have the effect of amplifying the emotional impact of the phenomenon.

Share What You Have To Offer With The World.

The benefit of being a part of a community is having people around us on whom we can rely for support as we make our way through the many stages of our lives. On the other hand, giving back to our community and finding opportunities to share our talents, knowledge, and experience with others may be extremely gratifying endeavors in and of themselves. The fact that providing value to others in a selfless manner can lead to the development of a profound sense of personal fulfillment is an intriguing phenomenon. The reward for being helpful to another person and assisting them in achieving their Ikigai is to experience this nice sensation and positive energy as a result of your efforts. When it comes to adding value to the lives of others, keep these three things in mind:

Have some guts, people!

In order to be of use to another person or organization, you will first need the bravery to step out of your comfort zone and realize the value that you, yourself, bring to the table. If you want to reach out to another person and share your skills, expertise, or talents with them, you might need the confidence to make the initial contact or take the first step in doing so. In a personal setting, this could mean having the bravery to offer guidance to a friend on a subject in which you have experience. In a professional setting, this could mean having the courage to suggest a new concept that can benefit the company or to offer your aid to a colleague who appears to be overwhelmed. Putting yourself out there might possibly have an effect that lasts a lifetime, and all it takes is crazy courage and twenty seconds of your time.

Please Don't Keep It to Yourself!

It's easy to take for granted how much information you have stored in your brain. This is especially true in situations in which you are surrounded by other intelligent people who might know just as much as you do and, as a result, might not appear to have any need for your assistance. However, the fact of the matter is that what you know can be helpful to other people who want to achieve the same things that you have been able to do. Finding others who are interested in being mentored or in having their knowledge shared is one way to grow your community.

Maintain Your Focus on Improving Yourself.

When you can't recognize the value you possess, you can't help other people in any meaningful way. In order to teach others about your abilities, knowledge, and skills, you must first have complete faith in who you are and acknowledge the value of what you bring to the table. How you look at yourself is important because it might be the factor that either enables you to extend yourself to others or prevents you from doing so. You will be able to add more value to anything you do for other people if you put the effort into figuring out your own passions and talents, as well as your own passions and limitations.

Debunked Theories About Anxiety

Are you one of those people who has been convincing themselves that they will get better on their own and that they do not require any assistance? If that describes you, then it's time to take a look at these 10 misconceptions about anxiety that I'm about to debunk completely. It's possible that the fact that you appear to be functioning normally is one of the factors preventing you from seeking the assistance you require. It is not uncommon for a person who is battling with an anxiety condition to give off the impression that they are nothing more than chronic worriers, rather than someone who may be struggling with a mental health disorder. Despite this, it's possible that your life isn't as fulfilling as the one you actually want it to be right now. Your decision regarding whether or not to seek therapy for your anxiety disorder will be heavily impacted by the severity of the condition you are suffering from. It is important that you read the following carefully since it may be the impetus you need to take the initial step.

There Is No Medical Evidence That Anxiety Disorders Are Real Illnesses

It's only natural that at some point in one's life, one may experience a certain level of anxiety; this applies to everyone. It can even be of great assistance at times. On the other hand, there are many who believe that you ought to have no trouble keeping your concern in check. They are speaking nonsense because they have never dealt with worry on the same level that you do on a daily basis, thus they have no idea what they are talking about. They are clueless to the fact that SAD can render you helpless in all aspects of your life. Anxiety disorders are a more severe type of the lighter, more fleeting anxiety that all of us experience on occasion. Anxiety disorders can be exceedingly debilitating, to the point where they seriously affect one's ability to make sound judgments.

If you have ever been given the news that you have a serious illness, like cancer, for example, you will have been subjected to a variety of diagnostic exams in order to arrive at that conclusion. Even though there are no physical tests, like as blood tests or scans, that a person can take in order to identify social anxiety disorder, there are a great many different ways that it can be discovered. That does not mean that it is a disease that does not exist because, believe you me, it does exist, particularly for people who are afflicted with it.

Attempted Suicide Induce you to pass out or cause you to lose control.

A quick drop in blood pressure can cause a person to lose consciousness, sometimes known as passing out. This does not occur when someone is having a panic attack. In point of fact, the reverse of what was expected occurs. Because a person suffering a panic attack will experience both an increase in their blood pressure and an increase in their heart rate, it is impossible for them to pass out during a panic attack because their blood pressure and heart rate will be too high. In point of fact, it is more likely that you will have a heart attack as a result of a panic episode than that you will pass out from lack of oxygen.

These assaults are terrifying not only to go through oneself but also to observe being carried out by another. One other compelling argument in favor of seeking therapy for anxiety disorders is that the fear of having a panic attack makes those attacks far more intense. It is possible that the fact that at least 20 to 25 percent of the population has experienced a panic attack at some point in their lives would be of interest to you. On the other hand, only approximately 2 to 3 percent of people who have panic attacks go on to develop a panic or anxiety disorder. This condition is characterized by a vicious cycle in which worrying about having the attacks actually makes it more likely that they will occur, and when they do, they will be more severe. Learning to accept panic attacks as normal and having the confidence that nothing negative would occur as a result of having them is an important part of the treatment for panic disorder. This factor alone has the potential to lower both the severity and the frequency of the episodes.

Putting Together Your Personal Protection Strategy

You will now have the opportunity to put your plan of action into motion. The majority of us put off beginning our exposures until we have to force ourselves to make time for them. To tell you the truth, facing one's worries is not a ticket to the amusement park; as a result, giving up the habit is far easier than keeping it up. If you give up your exposure sessions in the here and now, it may mean that you will have to learn to live with dread and anxiety in the future. The dangers posed by exposures are frequently exaggerated in people's minds. When someone engages in exposure exercises on a more regular basis, they increase their likelihood of making a speedier recovery from their mental disease. As an illustration, a person could list the activities of answering phone calls, going to the grocery store, and relaxing in her garden as the first three exposure activities that she had. These therefore become the principal objectives of the many exposure events that are to be faced. Determine the exact day and time that you will undertake your first practice session of exposure, and then move on to the next step. Making a definite time commitment to yourself can help you complete the task. In addition, schedule periods when you will repeat an equivalent exposure session, as repetition is an essential component in conquering fears and phobias. If at all feasible, you should avoid leaving a gap each day between the two times you repeat something. The exposure sessions should take place as frequently as possible. The amount of time that should be spent in an exposure work will most likely vary from person to person; nevertheless, a good rule of thumb is to stay in the situation until the anxiety has substantially subsided (by roughly fifty percent).

Being Practical Regarding the Probability of Unfavorable Occurrences

People who struggle with anxiety issues tend to have an irrational fear of negative outcomes and the tendency to incorrectly believe that these outcomes are extremely likely to occur. If a person is anxious about being ill, being hurt themselves or their loved ones, having a frightening experience, or being shunned by their peers, that person tends to exaggerate the likelihood that any of these negative outcomes will occur. Anxiety can have a significant impact on your ability to reason and think clearly.

Putting Negative Events and Activities into Perspective

People who suffer from anxiety are more likely to exaggerate the severity of a feared scenario in their minds than they actually are in real life. Anxiety causes a person to have a tendency to exaggerate the significance of unfortunate or unpleasant occurrences, and as a result, they may come to the conclusion that these things are intolerable, terrible, or the end of the world.

The good news is that bad things hardly never happen. The majority of the time, a person will confront their feared situation regardless of how challenging or unpleasant it is going to be. Increased beliefs in our capacity to deal with unpleasant experiences and sensations are at the heart of anti-anxiety ways of thinking. These ways of thinking can help reduce feelings of worry and stress. Even though coping with anxiety is not an easy task, you should always reassure yourself that you are capable of doing so and that you will. Keep in mind that you have survived previous periods of panic and anxiety, despite the fact that you found those times to be extremely uncomfortable and that you went through them. You are also going to work on creating improved attitudes towards the chance that other people may judge you in an unfavorable way. It is best not to place an excessive amount of emphasis on what other people might be thinking about you because this could cause you to feel even more scared and anxious than you already are. Instead, you should constantly remind yourself and maintain an attitude that goes something like this: "it is unfortunate if people think negatively about me, but it is not unbearable or terrible." Keep in mind that despite how humiliating your symptoms of hysteria may also be, other people may be more tolerant and caring toward you than you would imagine. Keep this in mind at all times.

: Practice Gratitude

One thing that has the power to alter the way you see things is gratitude. This is the crux of the matter. When you are experiencing anxiety, your thoughts will typically focus on all of the annoyances and anticipated failures that you are imagining. But thankfulness directs your attention to the successes you've achieved and the positive aspects of your life. It opens your eyes to the fact that not everything is drab and dismal. Your fears will diminish to the extent that you are able to cling to that sensation.

Being grateful draws your attention to the here and now. It redirects your attention on the things that you already possess and enables you to take pleasure in the present moment. It is challenging to have an attitude of gratitude since it makes it more difficult to take things for granted. As a result, you will find that you are concentrating more on cultivating real relationships rather than paying attention to every insignificant detail that means less. Having an attitude of thankfulness is necessary for this reason. Just stop what you're doing for a second and soak in all of thesplendor that surrounds you. Instead than focusing on the negative aspects of a situation, try to find the positive aspects. Also, don't forget to express gratitude to those around you and let them know how much you value them. This little action will calm you down and assist you in regaining your equilibrium.

Both The Cortex And The Amygdala Are Involved.

There is a good chance that you are already familiar with the cortex, which is the portion of the brain that occupies the top part of the skull. It is the part of the brain that is responsible for thinking, and some people believe that it is the part of the brain that is responsible for making us human. This is because it enables us to reason, form language, and take part in complicated speculation, such as logic and mathematics. People have a tendency to attribute a higher level of intelligence and sagacity to the kinds of animals that have larger cerebral cortices.

There are a number of different approaches to treating anxiety that center on the cortical route. These approaches typically revolve around cognition, which is the mental term for the psychological processes that the vast majority of people refer to as "thinking." Thoughts that originate in the cortex have the potential to either be the cause of anxiety or to have the effect of either increasing or decreasing anxiety levels.

Altering our medicine can help us in certain situations to prevent our mental processes from beginning to contribute to anxiety or from beginning in the first place.

A lesser amount of consideration had been given to the amygdala pathway by anti-anxiety medications up to this time. The amygdala is a relatively small structure, yet despite its size, it contains thousands of distinct cell circuits that are each responsible for a different function. These circuits have an effect on love, sexual behaviour, anger, hostility, and fear. The amygdala's function is to create emotional memories as well as to assign emotional importance to events or things that have occurred in the past. The sentiments and memories associated with those emotions can be either pleasant or negative. In the following discussion, we will focus on the ways in which the amygdala links experiences to feelings of anxiety and creates memories that are anxious-provoking. You will have a better understanding of the amygdala as a result of this, which will make it easier for you to determine how to modify its circuits in order to reduce anxiety.

We humans aren't purposefully aware of the way in which the amygdala connects anxiety to circumstances or things, just as we aren't deliberately aware of the role that the liver plays in digestion. In any event, the emotional programming that occurs in the amygdala has an effect on our behavior. The amygdala is at the very center of where the anxious response is generated, as will be elaborated upon throughout the course of this study. In spite of the fact that the cortex can either initiate or contribute to anxiety, the amygdala is necessary in order to initiate the anxiety response.

Because of this, addressing anxiety in a comprehensive manner entails addressing both the cortical circuit and the amygdala pathway simultaneously.

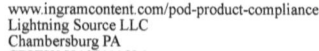

www.ingramcontent.com/pod-product-compliance
Lightning Source LLC
Chambersburg PA
CBHW052135110526
44591CB00012B/1734